My Guide Inside

Knowing Myself and Understanding My World
(Book I)
Learner Book

Christa Campsall
with
Kathy Marshall Emerson

3 Principles Ed Talks
myguideinside.com

© 2018 Christa Campsall; updated 2020 www.myguideinside.com

My Guide Inside® is a registered trademark of Christa Campsall (3 Principles Ed Talks)
ISBN-13: 978-1981469253
ISBN-10: 1981469257
Library of Congress Control Number: 2017919712
BISAC: Education/Students & Student Life
CreateSpace Independent Publishing Platform (a subsidiary of Amazon.com)
Charleston, SC

All rights reserved. No part of this work covered by copyrights hereon may be reproduced or used in any form or by any means—graphic, electronic or mechanical—without the prior written permission of the author, except for reviewers who may quote brief passages. Any request for photocopying, recording, taping or storage on information retrieval systems for any part of this work shall be directed in writing to the author at myguideinside.com

E-books, MGI Online, Video on Demand Classes, Video Clips, and Digital Media Tools: See www.myguideinside.com for information on these resources.

First Printing, 2018
Printed in the United States of America
Authored With: Kathy Marshall Emerson
Conceptual Development: Barbara Aust and Kathy Marshall Emerson
Design: Josephine Aucoin
Production: Tom Tucker
Webmaster: Michael Campsall
Stock Images: Shutterstock

Why an Owl? Over the years as a classroom teacher, Christa was given various owl gifts. She loves them as symbols of the wisdom we all share. Starting in ancient times and throughout history, various cultures have seen the owl as linked with wisdom and guidance. The owl's big, round eyes symbolize seeing knowledge. Although it is sometimes linked to other ideas, it is because of this connection to wisdom, guidance, and seeing knowledge that the owl was chosen as the graphic symbol for *My Guide Inside (MGI)*. Christa hopes this interpretation is also meaningful to you. One of her former students, Jo Aucoin, now a graphic artist, was commissioned to create the *MGI* owls and clouds graphics.

Table of Contents

What Kids Say They Learned iv

Chapter 1 Discovering My Guide Inside 2

Chapter 2 My Feelings Come from Thought 8

Chapter 3 Happiness Inside Me 16

Chapter 4 Fast and Furious or Calm and Curious 23

Chapter 5 Enjoying Friendship 30

Chapter 6 Being A-Okay Today 37

Chapter 7 Seeing and Helping Others 44

Chapter 8 Knowing Myself 52

Chapter 9 Dandy Words 56

Overview and What Teachers Say 59

Note: *My Guide Inside Learner Book I* is written at Grade 2/3 reading levels. Parts of this book have also been used successfully with K/1 classes. Teachers are encouraged to use *MGI* as a resource and adapt or modify as needed. Some pages are included on the *MGI* website (myguideinside.com) for optional classroom large screen projection.

My Guide Inside® (Learner Book I)

What Kids Say They Learned

✣ "Wisdom whispers to me."

✣ "The best thing I learned from my guide inside solved all my problems. And my problem was I worried too much."

✣ "I learned to listen to my little voice inside."

✣ "I learned that everyone has a guide inside them. If you use it you will do the right choice."

✣ "I have learned to not get involved in conflict."

✣ "Being a good friend even if we disagree."

✣ "The best thing I learned was stay calm and curious instead of fast and furious."

✣ "The best thing I learned was holding onto bad [thoughts] is not good."

✣ "The best thing I learned was to get rid of bad [thoughts]. I let them go."

✣ "That the sun behind that bad cloud is always shining."

✣ "I can control myself and be less distracted."

✣ "I trust what I think and feel good about it. I am feeling more brave. You have to trust and be brave."

✣ "The best thing I learned was being a-okay is natural."

1. Discovering My Guide Inside

"Who wants to leave the nest? Fly from our tree?" Mama Owl asked.

"Not me!"

"Not me! Not me!"

"One day you'll be ready; one day you will fly."

"When?" squeaked Hooty as Peep declared loudly, "Not now!"

"You will know when, and you will know how! Just listen inside.

My Guide Inside® (Learner Book I)

Chapter 1
Discovering My Guide Inside

Come on along!

> **Let's learn something new:**
>
> You have a guide inside.
> It is wisdom and common sense.
>
> Everyone has this guide inside.
> Just look for the feeling.
>
> You can trust your guide.
> It points you the right way.

Learn to know yourself and your world. It's fun to discover your guide inside! This guide is always with you. You were born with this gift of wisdom.

Answer a Riddle
What is it?
It is not in the past.
It is not in the future.
It is always present.
You cannot touch it, see it, or put it in a box.
You know it by the good feeling.
We all have it.
What is it?

Your Precious Guide

You have a guide inside. It is wisdom and common sense. Your guide is full of insights. Insights are helpful new ideas. All you need to do is notice.

What happens when you do?

**As we live in our world,
24 hours a day,
7 days a week,
365 days a year,
(24/7/365),
Wisdom is present!**

Everyone has this guide inside. Just look for the feeling. When you are calm, you notice a good feeling. Then it is simple to listen to your wisdom.

You can trust your guide. It points you the right way. You will know what to do.

My Guide Inside® (Learner Book I)

Think of a Time

When you were little did you always take something special with you? Did you sleep with it?

Evan always took Buffy—a buffalo stuffie—with him. Sometimes the little buffalo was missing. Evan cried and screamed until it was found.

One day Evan's parents drove him to the park. He was so happy to see all the kids. Evan ran off to play. He forgot Buffy in the car.

Evan loved playing with the kids. He did not think about Buffy at all! After that Evan did not always carry Buffy with him. He knew it was okay to leave Buffy when he went to school.

Evan always kept Buffy in his room at home. Sometimes he still took Buffy to bed with him. Evan was starting to be secure no matter where Buffy was.

Did something like this happen to you? Or do you know a boy or girl who is like Evan?

Your guide inside helps you grow up.

Reading Responses

Chime In
What is your guide inside?
What is your best name for it?
How does your guide inside help you?

My Guide Inside® (Learner Book I)

Connect What You Know
"Just look for the feeling. When you are calm, you notice a good feeling. Then it is simple to listen to your wisdom."

Think of a time you were calm and noticed a good feeling.

Wonder
Be curious! Explore these helpful points:
You have a guide inside. It is wisdom and common sense.
   Everyone has this guide inside. Just look for the feeling.
   You can trust your guide. It points you the right way.

Create Your Journal
Make a journal for your reading responses. Draw a picture of yourself on the cover.

Show You Understand
Think of a time you were happy. Were you doing something you liked? Were you active or quiet? Write or draw about this happy time in your journal. Make sentences, draw a diagram, or use your own idea.

Ask an adult to help you
See the "Resources Tab" at myguideinside.com for extras. See Video On Demand to bring this chapter to life! Password: mgi

Activities

Create Big, Bright, and Beautiful Art
What do you imagine your guide inside is like?

Draw a picture. Use your own unique idea.
Title it: "My Guide Inside is Like…"
Display your art to see all the different ideas the group has.

Play and Have Fun: Listen to Stay in the Game
To stay in the game, only do actions when you hear, "Simon says." Examples are: act like a puppy, cut like scissors, do a happy dance, draw with your feet, gallop like a horse, hug yourself, play air guitar, and stand on one leg like a heron.

How did your guide inside help you stay in the game?

Dandy Words

These are very good words to know and use.

Calm—peaceful, quiet, still
Common sense—knowing to make good choices, insight, my guide inside, wisdom
Create—make
Curious—interested
Feelings—thoughts in action, happen inside you
Happy—feeling glad
Insight—a helpful new idea, common sense, my guide inside, wisdom
Listen—hear deeply, as "listen with your heart"
My guide inside —common sense, insight, my wisdom
Notice—see, watch for
Precious—valuable, very important
Present—with you, inside you
Secure—feeling good, safe, at ease
Thought—my power to think, create ideas
Wisdom—knowing what is true or right, common sense, insight, my guide inside
Worried—upset, scared, troubled

2. My Feelings Come from Thought

When you clear unwanted weeds, garden plants grow.
If I clear my unwanted thoughts my good feelings show.
Notice your own good feelings today!

Chapter 2
My Feelings Come from Thought

Come on along!

In Chapter 1 you discovered your guide inside. In Chapter 2 get ready to learn your feelings are created by your thoughts.

> **Let's learn something new:**
>
> My thought creates my feeling.
>
> All my feelings come from thought.
>
> I let unwanted thought pass by, and well-being is present.

Alice and Ed's Story

Alice and Ed share a lot! They have exactly the same room, house, family, and pets. They are in the same classroom at school. They even share the same birthday.

Do Alice and Ed ever have exactly the same day?

Alice's Day

Alice feels upset and worried. It is her turn to "show and share" at school. Ms. Jackson calls on Alice to share. She does not move. She just looks down. She feels scared.

Alice is still feeling upset when she gets home. Her kitten, Munsy, chews on a toy. Alice yanks the kitten's tail. Munsy hisses and runs under the bed.

After supper Grandma and Mama clean up. Mama asks a little riddle. "Imagine you want to get out of a room that has no door and no windows. What will you do?"

Alice's eyes light up. She giggles and says, "Stop imagining it!"

Ed's Day

Ed goes to the store with Grandma after school. He begs for a treat, but Grandma says, "No!" Ed feels angry and erupts like a volcano. On the walk home, Ed hides behind Grandma and will not say hello to her friend.

After supper Ed is busy writing in his book. Ed looks up and sees his little brother fall. Ed gently picks him up. He gives the baby a hug.

A Little Secret
Before long Grandma calls out, "Ed! Alice! It's time for bed." The twins get into their beds. Grandma says, "Tell me about your day."

"Oh, Grandma, Alice was feeling upset. After supper Mama asked her that funny riddle. Alice just got silly and happy again," Ed says.

Alice jumps in. "I know Ed felt angry about not getting a treat. I saw he was nice to the baby tonight."

Grandma chuckles. "I see both of you are wise. I'll let you in on a little secret. My thought creates my feeling. All my feelings come from thought. All of your feelings come from your own thoughts."

My thought creates my feeling.

"So?" Ed asks.
"So what?" Alice says with a puzzled look.
"So you can have a stormy time or a sunny, calm time. Let unwanted thoughts pass by, and your well-being is present," Grandma explains.

"I had lots of well bean today!" Alice says proudly.
Grandma laughs. "I said well-being. It means feeling a-okay."
"Ohhh! Well-being!" Alice repeats while Ed giggles.
"What was the best part of your day?" Grandma asks.
Alice says she loved the riddle. Ed says it was hugging his baby brother. He asks, "Grandma, can we have a hug now?"

Grandma holds them close. She says softly, "You don't have

to worry. Know you can be happy. Know I love you no matter what!"

Know you can be happy.

Well-being Is Present

The next night Grandma asks Ed and Alice about their day again. They both think the day was better.

Grandma smiles. "Here's a simple secret: listen to your guide inside. This little voice of wisdom helps you let go of unwanted thoughts. What have you noticed today?"

"Well, I don't need to erupt like a volcano when I don't get what I want," Ed admits.

"And I don't have to think like a scaredy-cat," Alice adds.

"How do you feel when you let unwanted thoughts just pass by?" Grandma asks.

"I feel more brave. Maybe I will talk in my class tomorrow," Alice says slowly.

"I feel happy!" Ed says.

"Now you know! Let an unwanted thought pass by, and well-being is present. It's true for me too!" Grandma tells them. "I wish you both sweet dreams. See you in morning town!"

Ed and Alice whisper, "See you in morning town!"

My Guide Inside® (Learner Book I)

Reading Responses

Chime In
Do Ed and Alice have exactly the same thoughts?

How did Alice feel when it was her turn to show and share?
How did she feel when she knew the riddle?
What changed?

How did Ed feel when he didn't get a treat?
How did he feel when he helped his little brother?
What changed?

What did you learn from this story?

Connect What You Know
"All of your feelings come from your own thoughts. So you can have a stormy time or a sunny, calm time. Let unwanted thoughts pass by, and your well-being is present."

Think of a time you noticed your well-being and were having a calm, sunny time. What were you thinking? What feeling did you notice?

Wonder
Be curious! Explore these helpful points:
   My thought creates my feeling. All my feelings come from thought.
   I let unwanted thought pass by, and well-being is present.

Show You Understand
Ed and Alice learned about well-being. How can this help you? Write or draw in your journal. You can make sentences, a mind map, or use your own idea.

Ask an adult to help you
See the "Resources Tab" at myguideinside.com for extras. See Video On Demand to bring this chapter to life! Password: mgi

Activities

Create Big, Bright, and Beautiful Art
Draw Ed's day. Fold your paper in half. On one half show Ed erupting like a volcano. On the other half show Ed helping his baby brother.
What changed? Everything!
Or
Draw Alice's day. Fold your paper in half. On one half show Alice acting like a scaredy-cat. On the other half show Alice laughing at a riddle.
What changed? Everything!
Or
Draw your day. Fold your paper in half. On one half show yourself having a stormy day. On the other half show yourself having a sunny, calm day.
What changed? Everything!

Play and Have Fun: Freeze Frame
We can care for each other. We can ask for help or we can give help.

Try this freeze frame drama game. Form two groups. If you are in Group 1 you need help. If you are in Group 2 you give help.
Freeze the action to show what each person is thinking and feeling.

Group 1 acts out being lost in a very hot desert and needing help. Freeze frame. You are lost in the desert. What are you thinking and feeling?

Group 2 acts out finding and helping the lost person. Freeze frame. You are helping the person. What are you thinking and feeling?

Group 1 group gets help. Freeze frame. You are getting help. What are you thinking and feeling?

Notice every person's feelings come from thought!

My Guide Inside® (Learner Book I)

Dandy Words

These are very good words to know and use.

A-okay—good, all right
Exactly—totally the same
Helpful—useful
Imagine—see something with your thinking
Love—care very much for, care no matter what
Scaredy-cat—a person who is afraid, shy, timid
Upset—worried, distressed, insecure
Well-being—feeling a-okay, healthy
Wise—full of insight
Worry—upset, feel scared

3. Happiness Inside Me

When clouds cover the sun, I know the sun is still in the sky.
As clouds pass by, I know I will see the sun again.
My cloudy thoughts also pass by. When that happens I feel happy. It's simple to see. Happiness is inside me!

Chapter 3
Happiness Inside Me

Come on along!

In Chapter 2 you learned your feelings are created by your thoughts. In Chapter 3 be ready to discover happiness inside you.

> **Let's learn something new:**
>
> I listen to my guide inside.
>
> Helpful thoughts pop up.
>
> My good feeling is present again.

Gail's Story

Gail was very happy when she was really little. Her big sisters loved playing with her. They didn't play with her much when she was older. Her sisters just told her what to do. Gail felt angry when they were unkind to her. She was always asking "Why?" and "How?" No one answered her. She was just the little kid.

Gail was the smallest at home. She was the biggest in her class. Gail started being mean. Soon no one wanted to be in a group with her. Gail was upset. Deep inside, she really wanted to be friendly. Mostly she felt angry and sad.

She really wanted to be friendly.

The class began to work on a project with high school Big Buddies. They planned to build a city using boxes, string, paint, and lots of fun things.

Gail was matched with a happy, caring buddy named Jayden. He could see Gail wasn't friendly at all. Jayden listened to his guide inside. A helpful thought popped up. "Maybe Gail just doesn't know any better."

Jayden was nice to Gail. He shared ideas with her. The nicer he was, the meaner Gail became. She snapped at Jayden. She even said his ideas were stupid.

In the first hour, Jayden and Gail barely started on the project. The recess bell rang. Gail made a beeline outside. She sat on the bench under the old oak tree. She looked up at the fluffy clouds passing by. She felt warm when the sun came out again.

After the break, it was Big Buddies time again. "What did you do at recess?" Jayden asked.

"I just sat under a big old tree," Gail said.

Jayden smiled. "What a great idea. Nature is everyone's friend!"

Nature is everyone's friend!

Gail made a face, but Jayden kept being kind. He looked at her and said, "I have something to tell you. It is so helpful. Will you listen?" Gail slowly nodded her head.

"When you were outside, maybe you noticed the clouds pass by. You felt the warm sunshine again. The same is true for you and me. Let unhelpful thoughts pass by just like clouds. Your good feeling returns. Can you think of ever being happy?"

Gail was quiet. She looked at her hands and said, "My sisters played with me when I was little. I was happy then."

"So you do know what happiness feels like! That's great. The good news is that you can be happy now!"

Gail scrunched up her nose. "How?"
Jayden looked into her eyes. "I know you can feel happy.

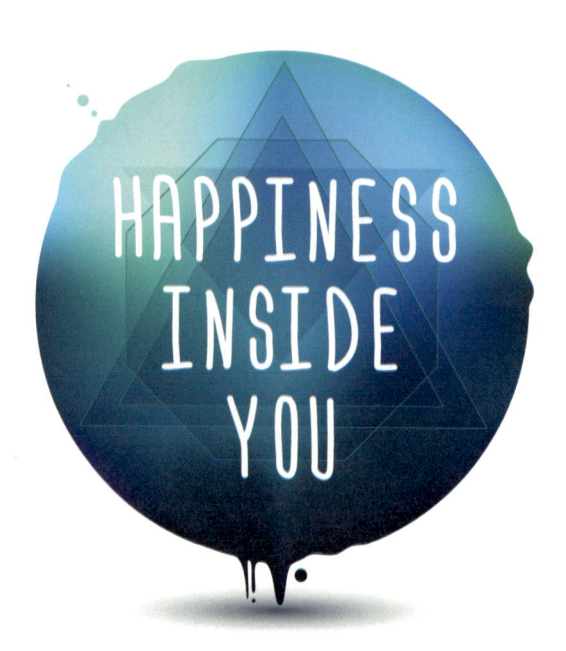

HAPPINESS INSIDE YOU

Happiness is inside every person. Happiness is inside you."
"Inside me?" Gail asked.
Jayden smiled. "That's right. Your thoughts just cover it up at times. Let the unhappy thoughts pass by. A helpful thought pops up. Your happy feeling returns!"
Jayden told Gail he read a book about a girl named Liza. "Liza's mom taught her that happy thoughts bring happy days, and sad thoughts bring sad days. I think that's common sense! Do you think so, too?"
Gail nodded. She felt relaxed and happy. Now she was curious about the project.
Soon, she and Jayden were sharing lots of ideas for making their part of the city. Gail told Jayden she went to a lookout at the top of a high-rise building.

My Guide Inside® (Learner Book I)

Jayden smiled. He said they could make a high-rise building. They could create a working outside elevator too. Gail liked that idea! She wondered how to do it.

They got a good start on their building before it was time to stop. Jayden said, "High five? Let's join the group now and share our ideas!"

Reading Responses

Chime In
What was the biggest change for Gail?
How will Gail treat her classmates now?
What does Jayden, the Big Buddy, hope you learn from Gail's story?

My Guide Inside® (Learner Book I)

Connect What You Know
"I know you can feel happy. Happiness is inside every person. Happiness is inside you."

In your own words, what is happiness?
How do you notice it? How does happiness feel?

Wonder
Be curious! Explore these helpful points:
   I listen to my guide inside. Helpful thoughts pop up.
   My good feeling is present again.

Show You Understand
Think what you would tell someone about being friendly and starting a friendship. Write or draw in your journal. You can make sentences, a list, or use your own idea.

Ask an adult to help you
See the "Resources Tab" at myguideinside.com for extras. See Video On Demand to bring this chapter to life! Password: mgi

Activities

Create Big, Bright, and Beautiful Art
Create in pairs. Show how cloudy thoughts like sadness "cover up" happiness.

Make a paper plate mask that looks like the sun.
Cut out the center so your face can be seen. Add paper triangle sunrays around the edge of the plate. Attach a craft-stick handle. Hold the mask over your face. Make your own face look sunny.

Then, cut out a cloud shape from colored paper. Write one or more words on the cloud to name cloudy thoughts. Add a craft-stick handle.

Take turns being the sun and the cloud. Move the cloud in front of the sun to show how cloudy thoughts cover up the sun. If you are the "cloud," you can also be the wind and blow the clouds away. The "sun" can call out sunny feelings when a cloud passes by.

Play and Have Fun: Happy Heart
Start with one child in your group lying on his or her back. Each child lies with the head on the last person's belly. Start with one person saying, "Ha!" the next person says, "Ha! Ha!" and so on. This creates a group belly laugh!

Did you notice a change in your thinking or feeling? What happened to the whole group?

Dandy Words

These are very good words to know and use.

Beeline—hurry directly to, run toward
Friendly—kind, nice, likeable
Friendship—bond between friends
Happiness—being happy, joyful, content
Kind—caring, helpful
Make sense—find meaning, figure something out
Natural—without help, true way, as in "being yourself"
Pops up—appears, as in "having an insight"
Relax—feel calm
Snap—speak with anger
Unhelpful—not useful
Unkind—mean, hurtful

4. Fast and Furious or Calm and Curious

Drop a heavy sandbag from a sailing hot-air balloon.
As its weight changes the balloon naturally lifts up.
If I drop my heavy thoughts, it is natural for my feelings to lift.
I feel lighter. I am calm and curious. A light heart is inside me!

Chapter 4

Fast and Furious or Calm and Curious

Come on along!

In Chapter 3 you learned happiness is inside you. In Chapter 4 learn you can choose to be fast and furious or calm and curious.

> **Let's learn something new:**
>
> I can see I am thinking fast and furious.
>
> I can choose to let it go.
>
> I can be calm and curious.

Kayla's Story

Today is the annual Children's Day festival. It is always very fun. Kayla is at home looking out the window. She jumps up and yells, "Mama's home!" Mama arrives home from work with a big bag of food.

"Mama! Mama!" Kayla shouts. She jumps up and down and pulls on her mother's arm. Tomatoes roll on the floor. "Oops!" Kayla gathers the tomatoes and drops them on the table.

Kayla grabs the dog's front paws. She dances in circles with the dog. Kayla is almost out of breath.

"When can we go to the festival? Will they have a bumper-car ride? Can we stay until the very end? Will they have cotton candy? Can I go on the hot-air balloon ride? Do we really have to take the baby? Do you think I will see my friends? Can I walk around with them? Will you let me? Will you? Will you?" Kayla says everything that pops into her head.

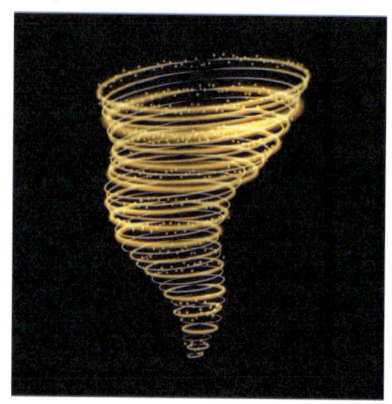

Kayla is still spinning wildly with the dog.
"Kayla, Kayla, please! You are talking so fast I can't even answer you. Look at the tired dog. Look at your baby brother. He is afraid you might step on him!"
Mama put her hands onto Kayla's shoulders. "Listen to me, Kayla. You have tornado thinking. It happens to all of us. I won't take you out to the festival when you are like this."
Mama looked into Kayla's eyes, "You can notice when you are thinking fast and furious. You can choose to let it go. You can be calm and curious. All the answers will come.
"We will have a great time. It's common sense to use your energy to help. You can help us get ready to go."
Kayla sees Mama is not mad. Kayla knows Mama is right. She lets go of the dog and just stops. "I have to go to the festival! Let's get ready. How can I help?"
Kayla helps Mama put the food away. Then she helps pack a bag for the day. Now they are ready to go. They hop on the bus to the festival.

Kayla calmly says, "Mama, I guess I was thinking like a tornado. Now I am just so happy we are going to the festival!"

Mama smiles. "Now you are calm and curious. Before you were spinning like a tornado. I am glad you used your common sense.

"We both have a new way to talk about being revved up. From now on we can help each other. Now I am curious to see what is at the festival. Let's go enjoy it!"

My Guide Inside® (Learner Book I)

Reading Responses

Chime In
How would the day have turned out if Kayla kept thinking like a tornado?
When Kayla is calm and curious, what does she do?
What is the important thing Kayla's Mama hopes you learn from the story?

Connect What You Know
"The best thing to do is use your energy to help."

How have you helped at home or at school?
How does it feel to be helpful?

Wonder
Be curious! Explore these helpful points:
   I can see I am thinking fast and furious. I can choose to let it go.
   I can be calm and curious.

Show You Understand
Think of a time you made the choice of letting thoughts go and were calm and curious. Write or draw in your journal. You can make sentences, a mind map, or use your own idea.

Ask an adult to help you
See the "Resources Tab" at myguideinside.com for extras. See Video On Demand to bring this chapter to life! Password: mgi

My Guide Inside® (Learner Book I)

Activities

Create Big, Bright, and Beautiful Art
Draw a picture of your own face on the bottom half of the page. On the top half, draw two big thought bubbles. In one bubble, picture fast and furious thinking. In the other, show calm and curious thinking.

First, share your picture with the group. Then, display it for others to enjoy.

Play and Have Fun: Thoughts and Feelings Change
Have you noticed your thoughts can change? You can change from thinking fast and furious to being calm and curious. Weather changes too. Sometimes weather is furious like a tornado and sometimes it is calm and still.

Put these pictures of the weather around the gym: cloudy, rainy, snowy, sunny, and stormy. Everyone starts in the center. The leader calls out one type of weather at a time. You choose how to move to get to the picture: hop, jump, run, tiptoe, or skip. Play music and have fun!

Have you noticed your thoughts can change like the weather? What does it feel like to have your thoughts change from stormy to calm?

My Guide Inside® (Learner Book I)

Dandy Words

These are very good words to know and use.

Choose—pick
Energy—power
Festival—celebration, fair
Furious—stormy, as "thinking way too much"
Naturally—in a natural way
Revved up—become very wound up, too active
Tornado—twister, as in "spinning thoughts"

My Guide Inside® (Learner Book I)

5. Enjoying Friendship

You and your friend look at the same sunset.
You think your own thoughts.
You each see the sunset in your own way. It is natural.

Chapter 5
Enjoying Friendship

Come on along!

In Chapter 4 you learned you can choose to be fast and furious or calm and curious. In Chapter 5 discover you can enjoy friendship.

> **Let's learn something new:**
>
> Friends have different ideas.
>
> My guide inside helps me listen to my friend.
>
> We both can have a change of heart.

Daniel and Jason's Story

Daniel and Jason are lucky! They met each other at school. They became good friends on the playground. Jason wanted Daniel to come for a sleepover. Their parents agreed. The boys were excited!

Daniel was full of ideas for the sleepover. He told his parents, "We will play my new game at Jason's house all night. We can build a space station. I will take my joke book too."

After supper Papa drove Daniel over to Jason's house. Daniel rang the doorbell. Jason came to the door. He was almost out of breath.

Jason said, "Dad and I set up the tent in the woods behind the house. We can play flashlight tag and eat weird snacks like fried grasshoppers. We will tell scary stories all night. Come on in!"

Daniel was in shock. His face got red. "That doesn't sound like any fun. Eating grasshoppers is weird. I'm going home!"

He instantly turned and ran back to the car. Daniel was upset. He was not staying!

Daniel said, "Drive away fast! Jason's plans are so bad. I can't sleep in the woods. There might be a wolf out there. Jason did not even ask me what I wanted to do."

Papa just sat there. He let Daniel talk but did not drive away. Papa said nothing. He just left it to Daniel to decide.

Daniel had many thoughts. "I know there must be scary things in the woods. I can't eat grasshoppers. They give me the heebie-jeebies! I really wanted to play my new game on Jason's big screen TV. I like him a lot."

They give me the heebie-jeebies!

Papa noticed Daniel settled back in his seat. Papa said, "Just be still for a little bit. It's like waiting for the signal light to change from red to green. The best ideas come when you are calm."

Papa explained, "It is natural for friends to have different ideas. You can listen to each other. Your guide inside helps you do that. It's common sense that you each might decide to change things a little bit."

Daniel said, "We really could have fun playing my new game. I know Jason just wanted us to have a good time."

"How about it buddy? Do you want to talk with Jason for a couple of minutes?" Papa asked.

Daniel had a change of heart. He said, "Well, now I kind of want to stay more than I want to go back home. "So, okay, I guess I will ring the doorbell again. Don't drive away!"

Inside, Jason's mom was urging him to check things out with Daniel. Jason was almost in tears and so unhappy. He just wanted a fun night with Daniel. Jason started to open the door to walk out to the car. Daniel stood there ready to ring the doorbell.

They were both surprised and grinned. "Jason, could we make a different plan? Maybe we could go in the tent some other time." Jason nodded. Daniel waved to Papa to bring his bags in.

Daniel did quickly look around the woods before they started to play in the house. Jason was really good at Daniel's game. Jason brought out all his weird snacks.

Surprise! The next morning, they asked for one more night so they could sleep in the tent. Both boys used common sense to have a change of heart. They are enjoying friendship!

Reading Responses

Chime In
Did they eat real fried grasshoppers?
What did Daniel's change of heart do to the sleepover plans?
What do you think the boys want you to remember about this story?

Connect What You Know
"Just be still for a little bit. It's like waiting for the signal light to change from red to green. The best ideas come when you are calm."

Think of a time you did this.

Wonder
Be curious! Explore these helpful points:
Friends have different ideas. My guide inside helps me listen to my friend. We both can have a change of heart.

Ask an adult to help you
See the "Resources Tab" at myguideinside.com for extras. See Video On Demand to bring this chapter to life! Password: mgi

My Guide Inside® (Learner Book I)

Writer's Workshop

Take Turns Interview
Interview each other. Remember when you made plans with a new friend and you both had fun.

You can be calm and curious to learn what ideas you each had. How did you decide what to play? What did you like best?

Making and Keeping Friendships Story
Every story has a beginning, middle, and end. Use your guide inside to help make and keep friendships. Write a story about a time you made plans with a friend, but you each had your own ideas.

What different ideas did you each start with?
How did each of you think about it?
Did you have a change of heart so you both had fun?
What did you each like best?

Write a draft. Use some of the dandy words you learned.
Get help with editing. Make a good copy of your writing.
Add a big, bright, and beautiful picture.

Read your story aloud. Include your story in the class "Making and Keeping Friendships" book.

Two Stars and a Wish
Re-read your story. List two things you did well. Name one thing you will improve in your next story.

Activities

Create Big, Bright and Beautiful Art
Draw and color what you think fried grasshoppers look like. Keep it secret. When you are done, compare your picture with the others.

Why is each picture different?

Play and Have Fun: Thoughts Change Like Signal Lights
Someone is "It". Their back is to the group. The group is on the other side of the gym. When "It" says "green light," everyone runs to touch "It." When "It" says "red light," everyone stops. If "It" turns around when saying "red light" and sees someone run, that person is out.

Repeat until everyone is out, or "It" has been tagged. Whoever tags "It" becomes "It"!

How did it feel to do one thing and quickly do something else? What helped you follow the fast directions?

Dandy Words

These are very good words to know and use.

Change of heart—a shift in thinking and feeling
Decide—choose
Heebie-jeebies—yucky, fearful feelings
Instantly—right away
Unique—one of a kind
Weird—strange

6. Being A-Okay Today

My thinking creates my feeling. This is how my world seems. I listen to my guide inside for insights. It is natural to feel a-okay!

Chapter 6

Being A-Okay Today

Come on along!

In Chapter 5 you learned you can enjoy friendship. In Chapter 6 you explore being a-okay today.

> **Let's learn something new**:
>
> I can have too much thinking.
>
> I can get stuck on a thought.
>
> I am a-okay with just right thinking.

Amy's Story

Amy is excited! She is going on a trip to visit her cousin Ella. Amy loves her cousin. Amy will celebrate her eighth birthday while she is there. She and Ella share the same birthdate. This year Ella will be exactly three times as old as Amy!

Ella is now an adult and so fun to talk with. She always has good ideas for things to do. As soon as Amy arrived, Ella had the idea to bike to the park.

Many kids were playing at the park. Amy stayed very close to her cousin. Ella sat on a park bench.

"Go have fun. I will watch you," Ella said.

"What if no one wants to talk to me? What if no one plays with me? What if they think I don't belong here? What if they are mean to me? Oh dear! What if…" said Amy.

Ella stopped her. "Whoa! You can have too much thinking!"

"I will be so sad if they don't like me. What if they do not like me? I should have stayed home where I am liked!" Amy moaned.

"Amy, you can get stuck on a thought! Come sit by me." Ella patted the bench. "You know the Goldilocks story, right?"

"What about it?" Amy asked.

Ella explained, "Goldilocks discovered the bowls of porridge were too hot, too cold, or just right. She found the chairs were too hard, too soft, and then just right. It's kind of the same for us in real life with our thinking. We can have thinking that's just right."

Ella said, "Too much thinking is fast and furious like a tornado. It is hard to know what to do. That never leads to fun!

"Too little thinking is being stuck on one thought. That doesn't lead to fun either!

"You are a-okay with just right thinking. When you are a-okay you listen to your guide inside. It is easy to notice helpful new ideas. These are called insights. This naturally leads to fun!"

"Okay, now what?" asked Amy.

You are a-okay.

"So, let's wait a bit. An insight can help you. I think you will know what you would like to do," Ella said. They both sat quietly and just watched the kids.

"I love the monkey bars," Amy said at last. "We did a lot of climbing and balancing in gymnastics last year."

"I am not surprised! I have seen you jump like a monkey. Think of jumping on my parent's bed when you were here last year. We laughed so much!"

"Oh yes! Aunty even got mad at you! She said you should have stopped me."

"That was a fun birthday party! Do you know what you want to do today?" Ella asked.

"Oh, I just had an insight! I will start with what I love. I want you to watch me. I am really good on the monkey bars now!"

I just had an insight!

Amy started climbing on the bars. She had fun hanging upside down and doing fancy balancing. Ella cheered her on. Before long other kids were watching Amy. They moved closer and asked Amy to show them her best moves.

Ella could see her cousin was having fun now. There was nothing Amy did to make that happen. It was natural. They just laughed thinking about jumping on the bed! Amy felt great. She was a-okay!

Reading Responses

Chime In

Amy was thinking too much when she arrived at the park.
What happens when you think too much?

How does Amy feel at the end of the story?
Describe feeling a-okay when you were at a park.

What would Ella like you to remember from this story?

Connect What You Know

"You are a-okay with just right thinking. When you are a-okay you listen to your guide inside. It is easy to notice helpful new ideas. These are called insights."

Describe a time you had a helpful insight.

Wonder

Be curious! Explore these helpful points:
 I can have too much thinking. I can get stuck on a thought.
 I am a-okay with just right thinking.

Ask an adult to help you

See the "Resources Tab" at myguideinside.com for extras. See Video On Demand to bring this chapter to life! Password: mgi

My Guide Inside® (Learner Book I)

Writer's Workshop

Create a Poem about Your Learning
Create a poem with one of these titles: "My Guide Inside," "My Common Sense," "My Wisdom," or use something else you have learned.

Think about the poem shape, pattern, feeling, and images.
Write a draft. Use some of the dandy words you learned.
Get help with editing. Make a good copy of your writing.
Add a big, bright, and beautiful picture.
Include your poem in a class poetry book, and add it to the class library.

Create a Poem about Your Life
Here are some things to choose from:

What you think about …
What you dream about …
What you care very much about …
What your image of happiness is …
What strong feelings you have …

Give your poem a title.
Write a draft. Use some of the dandy words you learned.
Get help with editing. Make a good copy of your writing.
Add a big, bright, and beautiful picture.
Include your poem in a class poetry book, and add it to the class library.

Two Stars and a Wish
Re-read one of your poems. List two things you did well and something you will improve in your next poem.

Poetry Café
Plan a fun Poetry Café to recite poetry for a group.
Which poem will each person practice reciting?
Who will speak first?
Will you use a microphone?
Who will you invite?
Will you have decorations and snacks?
Will you have a place for guests to write what they enjoyed?

Have fun! Take time for everyone to say how it felt to recite their poem.

Activities

Create Big, Bright, and Beautiful Art
Make a heart-shaped map of the people and things you love.
How do you feel making your map?

Play and Have Fun: Choose What Feels Right
Play on the playground. Notice all the different play choices. Kids choose what feels right to do. Follow your guide inside. Find what feels right for you and join in the fun!

Dandy Words

These are very good words to know and use.

Choice—freedom to choose
Dream—think up, imagine
Stuck—jammed, unmoving

7. Seeing and Helping Others

I am feeling a-okay. I see when someone needs help.
I listen to my guide inside and know to give help or get help.
It is simple to notice. It is natural to do.

Chapter 7
Seeing and Helping Others

Come on along!

In Chapter 6 you learned it is natural to be a-okay today. In Chapter 7 be ready to discover seeing and helping others.

> **Let's learn something new:**
>
> When I am feeling a-okay,
> my thinking is calm and curious.
>
> I notice when someone needs my help.
>
> My guide inside helps me to know what to do.

Owen and Nathan's Story

Owen feels a-okay most of the time! He and his classmates learned to listen to their own guide inside. Listening for insight helps each of them know what to do. They are mainly calm and curious now.

It is natural to be kind, friendly, and helpful—in class, on the playground, and at home. The students find caring and sharing is easy. They see when someone needs help. Everyone needs help sometimes.

Caring and sharing is easy.

Owen notices when he feels good. Owen also can notice when he is not feeling okay. He listens to his guide inside. Soon he is back to feeling happy. Owen says it's true for everyone.

Owen sees when someone else needs a little help. He watches Nathan who lives nearby. He is two years younger than Owen. They both love playing soccer. Almost every day they kick the ball back and forth. Owen has played on a team for two years. Nathan is just beginning.

At first, Nathan was happy to join the team. Then he asked, "What if I am not as good as the other kids?" Owen sees Nathan needs help. Owen has an insight! He asks to go along to Nathan's first practice game. Nathan slowly says, "Well, okay. At least I know you are my friend."

They walk to the practice. Owen explains, "When I first started soccer, I just watched and watched. My dad told me practicing was the way to get better. I was so scared. My legs were kind of frozen, but I knew my dad was right. Now I know playing is way more fun than just thinking about the other kids!"

Playing is way more fun than just thinking!

"You practice a lot. Now you're so good. Your dad is right!" Nathan added.

Nathan watched the first half of the game. It was his turn to go on. "The other new kids are much better at this. I don't want to play!" he whispered loudly to Owen.

Owen quietly said, "Just wait a bit. See how you feel. You will know how to play. When I started on a team, I kept falling over the ball. I laid on the grass more than I kicked the ball!"

Nathan looked down and shuffled his feet. He ran to the field just as the game started again. The players ran up and down the field. Nathan made a great pass, and his teammate got a shot on goal!

Now Nathan was defending. The player on the opposite team made two quick moves. Nathan fell smack onto the grass! The player scored. Nathan's face turned red. He really wanted to go off the field.

When the whistle blew, he ran over to Owen. "Did you see me? I can't do this!"

Owen looked at Nathan, "Well, it might feel bad to get beaten in that play. I've seen you get over it when we play at the park. You can do it on the soccer field too."

Nathan caught his breath. "You want me to just get over it?"
Owen added, "That's up to you. I know soccer is fun!"
"Well, I really do want to play," Nathan replied.
"You don't have to stay in the game. If you do stay in the game, feel a-okay about it! That's when you play your best," said Owen.

They walked home after the game. Owen told Nathan, "Your pass to the forward was awesome! He got a shot on goal because of you." Nathan looked up at Owen and smiled.

Owen told Nathan, "My dad says we can practice and be a

good team player! Sometimes I still get upset like a tornado. I get over it and I feel good again. I really like being on a soccer team. So do you want to practice with me tomorrow?"

Nathan scrunched up his face. "I do want to get better! And I like to practice with you. Yes!"

My Guide Inside® (Learner Book I)

Reading Responses

Chime In
Nathan thinks only about his missed pass. How does he feel?
How does Nathan feel if he thinks about his awesome pass?
Will Nathan stay on the team or quit?
What does Owen hope you will learn from this story?

Connect What You Know
"It is natural to be kind, friendly, and helpful—in class, on the playground, and at home. The students find caring and sharing is easy."

What do you know about caring and sharing?

Wonder
Be curious! Explore these helpful points:
When I am feeling a-okay, my thinking is calm and curious. I notice when someone needs my help. My guide inside helps me to know what to do.

Ask an adult to help you
See the "Resources Tab" at myguideinside.com for extras. See Video On Demand to bring this chapter to life! Password: mgi
learning, doing, and helping.

My Guide Inside® (Learner Book I)

Writer's Workshop

My Storybook
You have a valuable story to tell. Write your story of belonging,
Write a draft for each part. Use some of the dandy words you learned.
Get help with editing. Make a good copy of your writing.
Add a big, bright, and beautiful picture to each part.

Cover Page: Include the title, a picture, and your name.

Inside Parts
Part 1: Belonging
Write about belonging to a group. What do you like about it?
Part 2: Learning or Exploring
Write about learning or exploring. What do you like about it?
Part 3: Creating or Doing
Write about creating or doing something on your own. What do you like about it?
Part 4: Seeing and Helping Others
Write about a time you saw a person needing help. Did you give help or get help for the person? What do you like about helping?

Two Stars and a Wish
Re-read your story. List two things you did well. Name one thing you will improve in your next story.

My Storybook Circle of Sharing
Which storybook page will each person in the group choose to read?
Who will read first?

Learners say one thing they liked about each story.
Have fun and enjoy each other's stories!
Place your book with the others created in writer's workshop.

Activities

Play and Have Fun: See and Help Each Other

Soccer: Play fairly and take turns while playing soccer or another sport.
Sandbox: Play together in a sandbox creating whatever you imagine.
Ball: With a partner, keep a ball up in the air.

As you played how did you help each other? What did helping feel like?

Dandy Words

These are very good words to know and use.

Belonging—being included
Defend—protect the goal
Practice—go over, prepare
Scrunched—squeezed
Seeing—understanding, noticing
Shuffle—move feet while feeling uneasy

8. Knowing Myself

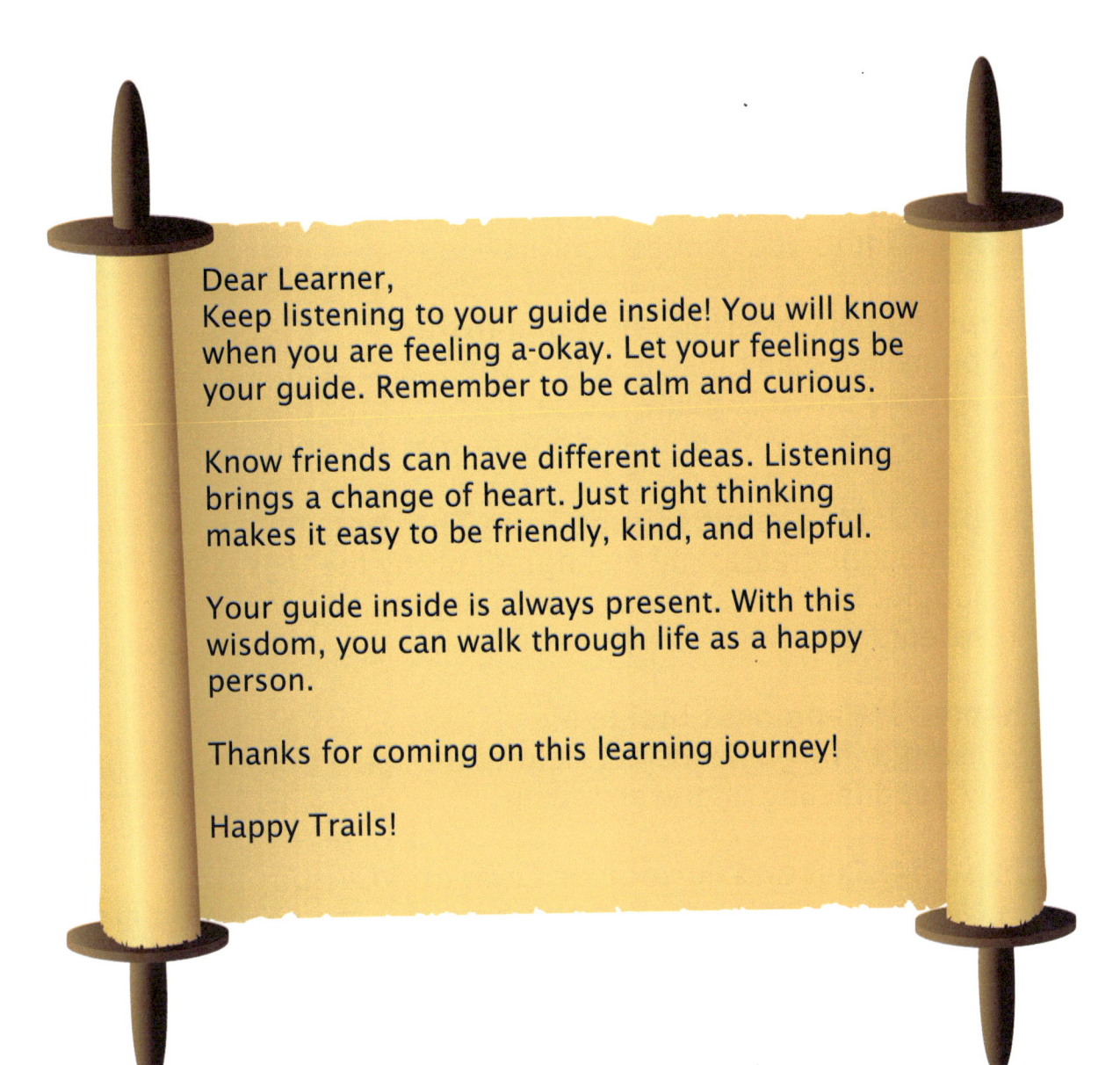

Dear Learner,
Keep listening to your guide inside! You will know when you are feeling a-okay. Let your feelings be your guide. Remember to be calm and curious.

Know friends can have different ideas. Listening brings a change of heart. Just right thinking makes it easy to be friendly, kind, and helpful.

Your guide inside is always present. With this wisdom, you can walk through life as a happy person.

Thanks for coming on this learning journey!

Happy Trails!

Chapter 8
Knowing Myself

Handy Reminders

Review a few chapters at a time. Each time you do this, say what is important to you. Notice your new ideas.

Chapter 1: Discovering My Guide Inside
You have a guide inside. It is wisdom and common sense. Everyone has this guide inside. Just look for the feeling. You can trust your guide. It points you the right way.

Chapter 2: My Feelings Come from Thought
My thought creates my feeling. All of my feelings come from thought. I let unwanted thought pass by, and well-being is present.

Chapter 3: Happiness Inside Me
I listen to my guide inside. Helpful thoughts pop up. My good feeling is present again.

Chapter 4: Fast and Furious or Calm and Curious
I can see I am thinking fast and furious. I can choose to let it go. I can be calm and curious.

Chapter 5: Enjoying Friendship
Friends have different ideas. My guide inside helps me listen to my friend. We both can have a change of heart.

Chapter 6: Being A-okay Today
I can have too much thinking. I can get stuck on a thought. I am a-okay with just right thinking.

Chapter 7: Seeing and Helping Others
When I am feeling a-okay, my thinking is calm and curious. I notice when someone needs my help. My guide inside helps me know what to do.

Activities

My Belonging Map
Ask an adult to help as you make your "Belonging Map." Draw a circle with your name in the middle. Trust your wisdom is helpful and always present. Sometimes you may need help from people you know.

Who could you ask? Think of a family member, friend, classmate, teacher, or someone in your community. Write these names around the circle.

My Dream
What do you dream you will do or be like? Write or draw about this dream in your journal. Talk about this with an adult you enjoy being with.

My Personal Poster
How do you like to think about yourself? Create a poster.

At the top of the page, write: My name is … and I am wise inside. Then copy and finish this sentence by adding more words: I am also …

Use as many words as you like. Some might be:

brave	happy	peaceful
calm	healthy	polite
caring	helpful	secure
cheerful	hopeful	smart
cooperative	joyful	strong
creative	kind	talented
friendly	lively	thankful
fun	loving	thoughtful
gentle	loyal	trusting
giving	patient	understanding

Below your sentences draw a big, bright, and beautiful picture. Create something that stands just for you.
Share your poster with the group. Display your artwork for others to enjoy!

My Guide Inside® (Learner Book I)

We All Have This Guide!

One day you'll be ready; one day you will fly.
You will know when, and you will know how!
Just listen inside. We all have this guide!

                                              Love, Hooty and Peep

Chapter 9

Words

Make sense of these words. These are very good words to know and use.

A
A-okay—good, all right

B
Beeline—hurry directly to, run toward
Belonging—being included

C
Calm—peaceful, quiet, still
Change of heart—a shift in thinking and feeling
Choice—freedom to choose
Choose—pick
Common sense—knowing to make good choices, insight, my guide inside, wisdom
Create—make
Curious—interested

D
Decide—choose
Defend—protect the goal
Dream—think up, imagine

E
Energy—power
Exactly—totally the same

F
Feelings—thoughts in action, happen inside you
Festival—celebration, fair
Friendly—kind, nice, likeable
Friendship—bond between friends
Furious—stormy, as "thinking way too much"

H
Happiness—being happy, joyful, content
Happy—feeling glad
Heebie-jeebies—yucky, fearful feelings
Helpful—useful

I
Imagine—think up
Insight—a helpful new idea, common sense, my guide inside, wisdom
Instantly—right away

K
Kind—caring, helpful

L
Listen—hear deeply, as "listen with your heart"
Love—care very much for

M
Make sense—find meaning
My guide inside —common sense, insight, wisdom

N
Natural—without help, true way, as in "being yourself"
Naturally—in a natural way
Notice—see, watch for

P
Pops up—appears, as in "having an insight"
Practice—go over, prepare
Precious—valuable, very important
Present—with you, inside you

R
Relax—feel calm
Revved up—become very wound up, too active

S
Scaredy-cat—a person who is afraid, shy, timid
Scrunched—squeezed
Secure—feeling good, safe, at ease
Seeing—understanding, noticing
Shuffle—move feet while feeling uneasy
Snap—speak with anger
Stuck—jammed, unmoving

T
Thought—my power to think, create ideas
Tornado—twister, as in "spinning thoughts"

U
Unhelpful—not useful
Unique—one of a kind
Unkind—mean, hurtful
Upset—unhappy

W
Weird—strange
Well-being—feeling a-okay, healthy
Wisdom—knowing what is true or right, common sense, insight, my guide inside
Wise—full of insight
Worried—upset, scared, troubled
Worry—upset, feel scared

My Guide Inside® (Learner Book I)

Overview of My Guide Inside® Comprehensive Curriculum
Contact: myguideinside.com

My Guide Inside is a three-part comprehensive Pre-K-12 story-based curriculum covering developmentally appropriate topics in an ongoing process of learning throughout the entire school career. As a teacher, you choose the level of My Guide Inside that is just right for your students in your particular school system: Book I (introduction, primary), Book II (continuation, intermediate), and Book III (advanced, secondary). This allows school leaders to chart a continuous instructional plan to share the Three Principles with students through the grades.

My Guide Inside, Book I offers Stories and Activities Designed for Success
- Ideal Participation Level: primary (age 4-8, Grades Pre-K-3)
- Reading Level: "very easy to read" (ages 6-8, Grades 2-3 level)
- Flexibility: regular course or adapt or modify to suit individual learners
- Settings: classroom, small group or individual
- Design: inclusive of self-directed learners working independently
- Digital Media: Resources at myguideinside.com
- Ideal Time: start of a program or school year to build community and foster optimism

Objectives of *Book I*: The principles discussed in this learner book operate in all people, including young children. This curriculum introduces the way to wholeness, happiness, creativity and well-being in all parts of life. Therefore, *MGI* has these two globally appropriate academic goals to: **(1)** Enhance Personal Well-being with an understanding of these principles, and **(2)** Develop competencies in Communication, Thinking, and Personal and Social Responsibility. *MGI* accomplishes both goals by using stories, discussion and various written and creative activities, as the learning increases your students' competency in English Language Arts and several other areas.

Discovering their guide inside is key to learning, and it enhances children's ability to make decisions, navigate life, and build healthy relationships. Accessing that natural wisdom will affect well-being, spiritual wellness, personal and social responsibility, and positive personal and cultural identity. Social-emotional learning, including self-determination, self-regulation, and self-efficacy, is also a natural outcome of greater awareness. This understanding maximizes personal well-being and improves school climate, learner behavior, and academic performance.

My Guide Inside® (Learner Book I)

Learning, Living, Sharing: The feeling a *MGI* teacher brings to the classroom every day, the "essential curriculum," is the greatest resource for directly impacting students. In other words, learning allows a teacher to live the principles by being in a natural state of service; sharing compassion, understanding and joy in the classroom. Once a teacher is being that informally and naturally, the teacher will be sharing the principles, via a positive feeling. This will enhance and make more powerful any formal lesson sharing with students. A teacher's own deep understanding and experience of these principles will bring out the best in all students. As each teacher continually learns and lives the principles, sharing this understanding with students becomes highly effective.

The *Teacher's Manual* for each book contains lesson plans, pre- and post-assessments, activities, evaluation scales, and resources. With universal principles, this curriculum is designed for global use with all learners. Curriculum guidelines from Canada, the United Kingdom, and the United States guide this work.

My Guide Inside® is available through myguideinside.com

Check the website for:
E-books, MGI Online for schools, Video on demand,
Resources, Translations and More..

***My Guide Inside®* Pre-K-12 Comprehensive Curriculum**

Campsall, C. with Marshall Emerson, K. (2018). *My Guide Inside, Learner Book I.*
Campsall, C. with Marshall Emerson, K. (2018). *My Guide Inside, Teacher's Manual, Book I.*
Campsall, C., Tucker, J. (2016). *My Guide Inside, Learner Book II.*
Campsall, C. with Marshall Emerson, K. (2017). *My Guide Inside, Teacher's Manual, Book II.*
Campsall, C. with Marshall Emerson, K. (2017). *My Guide Inside, Learner Book III.*
Campsall, C. with Marshall Emerson, K. (2017). *My Guide Inside, Teacher's Manual, Book III.*
Picture Book (Pre-K)
Campsall, C., Tucker, J. (2018). *Whooo ... has a Guide Inside?*
Supplemental Books for Parents and Educators
Marshall Emerson, K. (2020). *Parenting With Heart.*
Tucker, J. (2020). *Insights: Messages of Hope, Peace and Love.*

My Guide Inside® (Learner Book I)

About the Authors

Christa Campsall (right) has a 40+ year legacy teaching the principles shared in MGI. This has been the foundation of her work as a classroom teacher, learning services teacher in special education and school-based team chair. She has a BEd and DiplSpEd from University of British Columbia, and a MA from Royal Roads University. Along with MGI curriculum development, Christa facilitates professional development for educators in the global community

Kathy Marshall Emerson (left), National Resilience Resource Center founding director, facilitates long-term school community principle-based training and systems change. Her free and globally available recorded webinar series, Educators Living in the Joy of Gratitude, features international veteran educators' outcomes of sharing the principles for as much as forty years in classrooms, school systems, and student services. She has a MA from the University of Southern California and is adjunct faculty at the University of Minnesota.

What Teachers Say about My Guide Inside®

I have been a teacher in underserved schools in Baltimore, Miami, and the Bronx for over twelve years. By sharing the simple understanding that students are able to decide how they wish to experience life through their choices about thought, I have seen aggressive students become peacemakers; shy, self-conscious children become confident leaders; and the level of consciousness and empathy raised in an entire school. I am thrilled that this curriculum will be seen and experienced by so many! This understanding has the power to change education and the school experience on a global scale!

Christina G. Puccio, Teacher, Mentor Teacher
PS 536, Bronx, New York, US

"I like the *My Guide Inside* stories that teachers could read and discuss. Consistent vocabulary from K-3 is useful so children can continue to use the knowledge and skills they learn from grade to grade as they move from one teacher to another. It is really wonderful that you put this together. I highly recommend adding your program to schools' zones of regulation for young children."

Linda Backerman Primary Teacher, Vancouver, BC, CA

My Guide Inside® (Learner Book I)

I was excited to share the information with the students. I added children's books that helped illustrate a specific learning objective. We would also talk about the principles throughout the day while working through second grade problems. I liked the activities and art projects

Primary Teacher, US

"This beautifully composed curriculum is a must for school principals, teachers, and teacher assistants. It points educators and their students towards a natural and inner state of well-being. All participants are given multiple opportunities to become learners in a state of joy and to access their common sense and innate wisdom in all areas of life. My Guide Inside is a holistic approach with the essence of our humanity at its core."

Dean Rees-Evans, MSc
Teacher, Researcher, Well-being Mentor, Macksville, New South Wales, AU

"Parents and teachers alike will find this a helpful resource as they work with children and youth to find the wisdom that lies inside each one of them, and to develop strategies for solving problems with the help of their own special guide."

Kelda Logan
Principal, Salt Spring Island, BC, CA

As a head teacher (principal) for over thirty years, I have often witnessed firsthand the restless struggles many children and youth experience as they begin to feel comfortable in their own skin. Christa's straightforward, simple but profound curriculum helps teachers to point youth in a different direction, to our guide inside, our essence, our wisdom. I would recommend this guide to teachers as a powerful source of support. It helps us all remember who we really are...pure love.

Peter Anderson, Cert. Edn. Adv. Diploma (Cambridge)
Three Principles Facilitator, Headteacher Advisor, Essex, UK

"These authentic stories are simple, yet profound, and have the capacity to lead students to their guide inside."

Barb Aust, BEd, MEd
Principal, Education Consultant and Author, Salt Spring Island, BC, CA

My Guide Inside® *(Learner Book I)*

My Guide Inside®
Comprehensive Curriculum

www.myguideinside.com

well-being
communication
responsibility
resilience
social emotional learning
relationships
academic success
self-efficacy
happiness

My Guide Inside (MGI)... designed to bring out the best in all students

Check out the other My Guide Inside Books!

**Whooo ... Has a Guide Inside? (Picture Book)
with Pre-K activities
My Guide Inside (Book I) Primary
My Guide Inside (Book II) Intermediate
My Guide Inside (Book III) Secondary**

For: Video On Demand Classes, Online Resources, E-books, MGI Online, Translations and More ...
myguideinside.com

Made in the USA
Columbia, SC
15 May 2024